Rituals for to Call Down Light

poems by

Amanda Rachelle Warren

Finishing Line Press
Georgetown, Kentucky

Rituals for to Call Down Light

Copyright © 2024 by Amanda Rachelle Warren
ISBN 979-8-88838-621-7 First Edition
All rights reserved under International and Pan-American Copyright Conventions. No part of this book may be reproduced in any manner whatsoever without written permission from the publisher, except in the case of brief quotations embodied in critical articles and reviews.

Publisher: Leah Huete de Maines
Editor: Christen Kincaid
Cover Art: H.N. James "Down By The Tracks"
Author Photo: H.N. James
Cover Design: Elizabeth Maines McCleavy

Order online: www.finishinglinepress.com
also available on amazon.com

Author inquiries and mail orders:
Finishing Line Press
PO Box 1626
Georgetown, Kentucky 40324
USA

Contents

Rituals to Stay You from Wander

Ridgerunner 1
Boneyfiddle: Floodgate 2
Communion Road (Resurrection is a Boulevard) 7
Burial Road...8
Ritual to Stay You from Wander..9
Unmarked Road 10

Rituals for the Tribe of Honey

Norfolk and Western: Powhatan Arrow..13
Dante Vena's Dog...18
Dear Wolfbrotherbrightnothing...20
Road Signs..21
Desire Road 22
Candy Run..23
You Can Destroy this if You Want...24

Rituals to Kiss the Saint of Understood

Dear Sister of the Resurrection 27
Sestina for the Wide Awake 28
Dear Empress of Raze, of Slash, of Burn 30
Gibbous Moon 31
Greenup Lock and Dam Road 32
Dear St. Matthew's Church..33
Blacklick Creek 34
Dear Shameful 36

Rituals for the Exorcism of Ghosts

Three Locks Road: Deadman Crossing 39
Loss as Mars 40
Something Else in the Snow 42
Dear Mother of Weakness 43
Bridge Road 44
Orpheus Road 45
Houston Hollow, Long Run Road 46
Magnolia, Salt, and Pine 47
Rose of Sharon: What Stays 49
Selves in Memoriam 53
In Amber 56
Divination Road 57

Rituals for to Call Down Light

Rases' Mountain Road 61
Judas Codex 62
Sorrow Road 64
Mid-Afternoon: Everything Darkens, Everything Bows 65
Shoreline 66
You Did Not Seem the Boy 67

for all'a'y'all

Rituals to Stay You from Wander

Ridgerunner

What pins us to the earth we can't yet name.
Sleeping through the summer's buzz, it might yet come to you:
        that humid sweetness, the snowdrift of pears shedding petals in the
light wind,
        and the guilt each creates in us brings which pain?

Each of us faces the pendulum of pull
countering the resignation to what breaks in us.

There is a grove of sweet grasses—nothing wrong lingers there.
There is a house of ghosts who kiss tenderly so as not to wake you.
There is a river which sings about the dark of stones.

There is the smell of woodsmoke or there is the murmur in the hall—
        bitter coffee in the evening hours.

There is the green hollow like a cradle of stained glass, and
there is the soft dry fall, and there are eyes like storms and skin
like stained maple and curses that read like promises
of blood and water embedded in the viscera of us all stirring
under the moon's insistence, and there are dagger teeth beneath
the fallen branches, and riots and sorrows and rains that smother
and swell and sweep everything cruel into your yard
where you stand
                flecked to the knees with what is stirred from silt,
or there is the world.

Which pain can you stand?

Leave and your stomach will churn with longing.
Stay and we will stay forever on the verge.
        Nothing in the dead of night will promise anything.

Just one more day, and I'll...
Just one more day, and I'll...

Boneyfiddle: Floodgate

> Save me, O God! For the waters have come up to my neck. I sink in the miry depths, where there is no foothold; I have come into deep waters; the floods engulf me. I am weary calling for help; my throat is parched. My eyes fail, looking for my God.
> Psalms, 69:1-3.

Where the rivers branch: Branch Ricky memorial. And where the rivers meet: the trellis, the catfish lure, my brother's golden name slowly effacing.

O, front porch Eden. O, wide mouth of river spilling into river. Floodgate.

We toe our sneakers in the bank of Ohio. We spit in the Scioto. We jostle South Shore, and scorn them there. Wild on our own bank: *God's country.*

We call it a mouth, though it do not speak. I expect you'd think none of it beautiful, what it might say.

Golden, kiss my wounds, ignore your own.

We learn these things in Eden: signing "I love you," how to smile like we were our own true brothers.

Floodgate a gag on that wide mouth.

When the barb of the hook enters the hand, we'll have a big problem.
When the barb of the hook enters the hand, it has to come out the hard way.

> Take a pull from the bottle, I'll pull it out slowly.

Hey, salvation! O, Seventh Street and wrathful Jesus. We don't drive through town like hell, because, dear Golden, this is God's country.

But if this is God's country, why don't they polish it nice,
all Sunday-shoe?

> Take a pull from the bottle, and we'll sing a church song.

When the spring flood comes, something is drowned in the roiling murk of it. Tick marks on the floodgate subsumed. Water seeps through the dark slabs of concrete slowly lifting the paint from the murals. Each year, more flakes off the face of the face we create to greet all others.

We hid at the mouth, not remembering from what. It is just where we come. Do not speak it. Do not. We cannot ask to be forgiven of this thing.

Golden, ain't our smile the same? Don't you recognize the faces that pass you on Front Street? Ain't we all cousin, brother?

There is no wrong cannot be righted. Every lean-to porch was beautiful enough to reason falling in love. At the floodgate we sat, shucking corn. Throwing silk on the water.

On the dirt bank of the Ohio, perhaps salvation? A smooth shard of green glass at the water's lip. A graveyard of pole props, broken y's.

Low, red cooler Eden. Eyes acetylene grey. Minnows $2.00 a mess in a Styrofoam bowl.

On the dirt bank of the Ohio. We scrambled over the floodgate, hid at the mouth. You named me. Fleur de lis. Blackbird. Trillium. Sweet Eden.

Two rivers flowed into Eden to water the garden, and there they joined at the mouth. The first river's name is Great and the second is Deer.

    What do you know about temptation?

Who named this ridiculous town? I laughed until I thought about loss. The things we abandoned, the nicknames we grew out of, or into.

    Do not speak it. Silence is. Sometimes as necessary.

O, Seventh Street Baptists, salvation's always two steps further. And hell may be, maybe, upon us. But Doris says she found Jesus on the back of her motorcycle, and God scowling in the corner of her kitchen saying: *Change your ways, kitten.*

    Aunt Doris says, *Golden*, she says, *Jesus forgives even us lousy sinners uninterested in salvation.*

What kind of motorcycle would a Christian ride? A Triumph.

Ask God why, re: the name of this town. Have her ask why.

My legs unfold on the bank like a family tree. My bones notched like a timeline. This town, this town. Golden, we do belong: bad teeth, Kool-Aid smile.

> Here the lot where my mother grew.
> Here a shell of the Ice House.
> Here the body shop, behind the Dairy Bar.
> Here the White Stallion.
> Here our lines cross.
> Here our lines cross.

After I left you they renamed Branch Ricky Alexandria Park.

> Blackbird, you are wrong. The park on Scioto Street was always Alexandria.

There is some sin in the slow pull of the river. Do not sing me that church song. There is quite a bit of sin in it.

> Did you pack up your care with your woe?

Everything—the undercut bank, the open grin of the summer floodgate, the ragged laurel along the path down to the mouth, the small stone wall of Alexandria, each broken bottle—we are is saying we belong.

> Take a pull from the bottle. Do not speak.

When you go, you will no longer know me. Flesh of my flesh. And the bank? The mouth? Thorns and thistles it shall bring forth to you.

Why there so many of us, Golden? Why we so scattered? We enter a bar and hit on our own cousin by mistake. Even when we go we find one another. Even when we return it is all at once. We cluster. We cling. When one goes down, they drag like an anchor, and us steadying a ship with no engine. That water is deep.

> Let me go.

      Jimmy pulled me over last week for speeding through New Boston past the coke plant.

When you take a fish off the hook be sure to flatten the fins in the right direction, move your hand back from the head. The spine of a catfish can cut your hand wide open.

What would you call them? Every living creature?

      Doris says, *The man gave names, but for the man there was not found a fit.*

You should not look at me that way.

      Pour some of that bottle on the wound.

Didn't we name each other? Didn't the water threaten the top of the floodgate? Doesn't it? They pretty it up a bit, a bit of paint, rename the park for a city of cultural value.

      Jimmy said, *Golden? I have a cousin they called that. Not a given name.*

O, wild note. Deep dawn. Burning sword. While he slept, God took one of his ribs and closed its place with flesh.

Ignore your own wounds. I can hardly see you in this light, Golden, where the river is widest, the sun set all low and round. We were drunk, a single beer from the low red cooler in the side yard, or that sweet homemade wine, sticky bottle, then the half-fifth. I can hardly see you, so many motes in the air. Stretched out on the bank. From this angle. Jesus. That burns.

When the hook. When it enters. When the barb of the hook. Please.

      Take a pull from this bottle. It won't hurt for long.

While you slept.
    While I slept.
Someone made of us the other's image.
    Stop looking at me that way.
I hold my hand to the sun—you are there

Do I speak you fair? Or do I, in plain truth say...
silhouetted behind the silhouette of my own hand against bright water.

The murals are new. But the oldest ones are already fading. Every year some of the river seeps through. That damp that seeps through anything. Renovations make it what it never was. A coffee haus. A brick-lined esplanade. I have a hard time remembering where it was. Massie? Scioto Street? This is not our revival.

Heathen, heathen blood, heathen blood. On my hand on your mouth on the water. Are we not each other's image? Did we not name the other? Golden, Shameful, and Lack. One was the only Shakespeare we knew. Not the one that stuck. Not the one I remember.

I says, *Yeah, Jimmy, me. Golden, me.* But he didn't let me go.

When the woman on the news covered the hundred-year flood. When she mistook a side-yard-fridge for one that had *actually floated out of someone's home,* I wondered if she would blame the swell for the bathtub of flowers in that yard on Massie. The floodgates just couldn't hold. I thought of you.

We made you a crown of thorns to match my catfish and hook stigmata. There was only one picture of Jesus in the Seventh Street Baptist. His heart exposed, somebody's valentine.

Wasn't John Jesus's cousin?
     He recognized him at the river.
He blessed him with his hands.
     And then he asked to be blessed.

Communion Road (Resurrection is a Boulevard)

For three days even the trees
have been dreaming of rain:
        leaves curl with want,
          roll and beg at dusk.

And for three days my bones have ached—
through the open window some note of longing,
        the seep of sky and damp, burrows—
        the clouds pass laden across the yellow churn of sky.

And heavy, everything a slow crawl.
        And dark, what sheen lay upon the night?

The rain does not come.
And you do not come, with a mouth
        as simple-sweet as the grass surrounding
        a church marquee that reads: *Patience is bitter, but the fruit is sweet.*

No one would think it an invitation
to put hand to latch. All doors lead to something; all doors
are an annunciation.
        In the hot-damp, the hot-sweet plenty,
        in the hot-ripe chirrup:
            I waits still 'til I hears my heart knock.

I dream of flesh cool and damp.
I dream the wheel and its soft shush.
I dream the sky
        cracking
into bright halves and everything
        suspended:
            field and body.

Burial Road

Above your small grave which reads
Baby Girl—December 29, 1935, yellow

roses in the chipped bottle fade.

Here, surrounded by my many dead,
it is always dusk and inevitable rain.

Dear Aunt Amelia, or Ramona, like every other child

you entered the world: (un)remarkably.
But you didn't last a day.

I imagine my grandmother's tears.

I do not know who leaves the yellow
roses now, since she too is dead.

As always, I come alone. I see no one.

And standing before your small grave,
I shove all my sorrow into your open mouth,

into the blue nothing of your body.

Ritual to Stay You from Wander

[Find the possum a point of contention.]
[Find St. Steven with hot lead and powder.]
[Find everywhere shunned and condemned.]
[Find the grit to scour my veins.]
[Find a tongue of poison to press.]
[Find catawba.]
[Find sugar.]
[Find them bright blue blossoms.]
[And gravity a ghost.]

Unmarked Road

Stay. Do the names of the dead not sound differently in your mouth?

What refuses to grant you passage?

You may wait, and the high grass will choke you.

What cruel earth rejects your body,
                                          what cruel heaven your soul?

Rituals for the Tribe of Honey

Norfolk and Western: Powhatan Arrow

> Entreat me not to leave thee, or to return from following after thee: for whither thou goest, I will go; and where thou lodgest, I will lodge: thy people shall be my people, and thy God, my God. Where thou diest, will I die, and there will I be buried: the Lord do so to me and more also, if ought but death part thee and me.
> Ruth 1:16-17

I go to bed with Golden on my mind.
Each morning, Golden on my lips. Arise.
Are you the angel they set before me?

    What are you doing here, Blackbird?

I tell myself there is no reason to go back, but if there is no reason to go back then there is no reason to stay away. What we learn from a logical syllogism never applies.

They called my momma Lil'Bit. A train ran through here. And Mamaw Toot, the train carried her all the way to Baltimore.

    What are you doing here, Blackbird?

It is fitting to make merry and be glad, for this your brother was dead, and is alive; he was lost, and is found.

If A, then why not A? If we need a lens in the filter of causation: therefore, therefore, therefore.

We are too old to wrestle some things to the ground. Acetylene grey, what lives like flecks in your eyes?

Golden, remember everything that marks me. The raised half moon on my calf. The crisp scar of the catfish's spines.

Acetelyne: little burnings, little lights which will not let me be.

A kind of darkness swelled in my chest for days.

The Norfolk and Western does not run through the railroad town. The railroad does not run through the railroad town. One blue truck sits: everything smashed, everything removed.

We gathered Job's tears, the dark grey berries; twisted out the stems; strung them on wire; draped them around the bedposts for luck.

She took the train all the way to Baltimore, fifteen. Married a man full of damage.

Maybe there is a flower consuming me, maybe those things.

    What are you doing here, Blackbird?

        Something is working like a splinter in a palm.

What I wanted to say was: call out *beautiful* convincingly

One blue truck sits, abandoned, at the station. No train will come. No one will come to take you home.

The wild horseradish grows. The bitter root. The many grasses between the ties. The chicory's blue blossoms over everything. And the jewelweed, bright with forgiveness, we called touch-me-not.

    Holy hold me, holy keep me and lie.

        Something is working like a stanza in a psalm.

    Be the shade upon my right hand.

The damaged man struck her, threw her down a flight of stairs. She came home.

And if we desire to see our blood separate, call itself a name? What will it remember as the song of its own becoming?

One week after marrying him she came home.

I am a loss, and together we are insequential. I mean, we do not follow reasonable order. No sum, but remainder: we are so far apart already, we can not be divided.

We don't talk, we just move.

There is always touch-me-not, but never honeysuckle.

I remember a name for myself like clear water in a clear glass.

> Here is my tongue, I mark it for you; it serves a god which lives in your skin.
> Here is my tribe, the tribe of honey; we have no rituals.
> Here is my skin, a pale traitor.
> Here are my lit eyes, fueled.

When I declared not my sin, my body wasted away, for day and night you are heavy upon me, and I am cut off.

> No one will come to take you home; the long whine of the train is not even an echo.

Don't talk, just move. The honeysuckle smells like something.

The heart we share is mistaken about certain things. I was not the one always leaving, you were not the one standing still.

Damaged, she came home. Amid a shower of sparks. A place behind the bar.

Must I always think distance? Must I always mouth remove?

> Move.

Once when Death had no vacancy, I came to stay with you. And if that's a great oneness, then whatever, whatever makes me whole.

> I am ashamed.
> My chest tightens in the dark when we walk blind.
> No moonlight in the valley, and your hand reaches.

And you can say it's love, but I am ashamed. I wanted to be you, but nothing in me is made the way you are made.

>   I pull you up the steep bank.
>   I hold the branch as you pass.
>   Kill the snake that raises its triangular head from the woodpile.
>   Scrape the sharp hoe the length of its long body.

Of course, I am ashamed.

Golden, there is never a right time to admit that once, while lying on your grandmother's couch in the afternoon, you tried to imagine each possible scenario leading to your cousin (distant, removed) growing hard against your naked thigh. Instead, you admit to admiring the image of a cormorant's u-ed neck on the faux-porcelain vase someone bought to "class up" the snow-on-the-mountain.

Yes, of course, that's what I must have been thinking of.

The route back is always longer. I wince on the gravel road. Soft-footed.

Golden, be my memory in remembrance of me. *I raise up the name of the dead, that the dead are not cut off from a place among their brethren.*

I have become the rumor. I am seen as a sign. And, Golden, if you had asked me, you could have left with me. I did not leave you behind.

Day and night you are heavy upon me. And the weight of your body? I remember.

>   If you asked, Blackbird, I would have resurrected you.

When we had dreams, when we had them, they weren't these.
I never expected to be so far gone.

During the drive between my book-filled apartment and the too-dear grocery, I caught the scent of us. And there, honeysuckle growing wild where none should be. Unexpected and throaty.

There is no salve, no sin; I trip through years like glass, amazed.

Become the lie I believe and you will be more than the better part of me I cannot return to.

> I dreamt of you, Blackbird, your mouth overflowing with honeysuckle.
> The scent made me sick. Every lip of petal curled out like a light.
> The sound it made. And I ran.

And you have marked me surer than Jesus marked the dogwood tree.

What do you tell your lovers, beloved, that you have signed your heart away to a past that never existed? We were never here. We name the unfulfilled for one another.

You smell of heat, you smell of rain, and the dark clay of the creek bed—those pockets of glacial moraine that make us foothills, though Rosemont rises above the strip mall like something slumbering, and the Great Seal stretches purple and dense halfway to the dipping handle of the drinking gourd.

> There shines, there, the dark slick of us.

My whole heart hangs on a bramble of some plant: flowerless, fruitless.

The crushed blossoms beneath our bodies, smelled like something. The damp of your back beneath my splayed hand, the damp of your chest against my resisting hand?

What are you thinking about, honey? I like that bird, it's real pretty there, Mamaw.

There was never a train to interrupt us along the track.

And if nothing but honeysuckle fills the air, I will choke on its brightness.

Golden, did you declare me dead forever and ever?

> What are you doing? Here, Blackbird.

How did I die, love? Where did they bury me?

The sharp twist before the peak of Rosemont is the only comparison.

> What you do to my body is obscene.

Dante Vena's Dog

24.7	2.2	Turn right, follow Blue Run Road.
25.4	0.7	Stop sign. Turn Left and proceed straight ahead.

> —*Geological Aspects of the Maysville-Portsmouth Region, Southern Ohio and Northeastern Kentucky: Joint Field Conference,* May 17-18, 1968.

24.7   The turn is imbedded, is a visceral memory. On the limestone arch, beneath the tracks of the coal trains,
a light blue cross, nothing else, no Jesus Saves[1].

In May, the snowmelt cuts beneath the sugar maple.
Copperheads stirring in the new warmth are broken stems
sending out their scent, their bright cucumber blossoming.

The slick shale of the creek stagnant in August.

24.8   There is nothing here that loves any more than the hard packed earth.

Blue Run is wishing it edged against a lake called Forgetful.
It dreams of quiet water. On either side the dark ridge.
On either side the fields that rim in bright corn rising.

25   To the right the stone, marked "Baby Girl,"
each year fades[2].
Frayed petals loosened from their plastic stems.

The shale splits along natural occurrences.
To the right the, not yet, stone of my father.

In the parlor, he sits, shining his gun. And the oil that spreads
against the chair scents each thought with silent punctuation.

25.2   The limestone grind in the yard is too heavy to move.
In it we rubbed corn into dust so fine it clung to our lashes.
They built the house behind it[3], they moved the road to accommodate it.

In the sun it glimmers with the bodies of fragile things.
If it is too heavy to move, who brought it here?
Who wore the deep furrow?

25.2   There is nothing below this earth but more earth.
When I opened the car door, Cesar ran. Straight into the only car to pass down the Run for days at a time. Except for mine.
Somewhere the shale is slick with blood beneath the cut road.

25.2   If no one comes, who is to blame for this chainless body?

1. In the railroad cut east of Minford, 28 feet of light-gray plastic, laminated clay is exposed which is thought to be a quiet-water phase.

2. Wheeler Cemetery is seldom tended. The chain-link gate throws out rust over the tall weeds. But there is a path that runs behind it, where nothing grows on the hard packed ground.

3. In the two-bedroom house with no running water; in the white two-bedroom house; in the white two bedroom house where I lay on the roof of the porch wondering about taps of cool water in summer, how to route a shower from creek water: 18 years of light, gray, I move through, exposed to nothing but sky.

Dear Wolfbrotherbrightnothing, Dear Darkness, Dear Gone,

The wolf is in his man skin, bristle-dark beneath pant-damp breath. You are betrayed (betrayal)—it is the smooth muscle of your neck, it is the roll of your body, the cut of teeth against the red lip, against the tall, glass bottles and the curve of hand smudged by flame.

Speak of the wolf and you come. Circle the windows. Lick the panes.
Ask the pollen bright moon for resistance.
I feign sleep.
I hear stepping feet in the dry grass.

You have replaced all wolves. And their children run wild along the creek beds.

I do not know what to beg for,
Blackbird

Road Signs

Each crabapple is lit:
little lamps in the bright sun.
In the night, we hold
a small light against
its smooth skin:
a tiny heart stilled, aloft,
the net of fibers within.

Desire Road

October bees, apple drunk,
      rub
            against the burst skins, baptized.

They are dying by droves against the chapel windows—
      smear
            the glass, spill into sills.

Candy Run

Shake the shadows of willow floss from your shoulders while I bless the backhoe driver brave enough to bury the body on the steep side of that there hill. The wash gravel of the service switchbacks rolls with every step. Halfway up, when our muscles scream against the calves of our jeans, pause

with a practiced face, glance down to elders who can't climb here with mercy. They shade their eyes outside the, god bless it, Candy Run Christian Union; nobody said nothing, but we walk in they place.

The pastor squint-stammered his eulogy into the sharp of sunset—asked us to, *think of his dear wife*. Try to memorize it: someone will want a full report of the send off. Ignore the sweat bee that sips against your elbow. Do not respond to the peony of pain soon to bloom there as fate makes of him a pocket of rot in the clay grit.

Once we gather like evening deer in the shorn grass, once we comment on the house's new lemon siding and redwood deck stain, once we eat fresh bologna on soft white loaf with freezer pickles and misery and whatever casserole in whatever Corningware, once we pretend to forget we didn't care at all (except of course, for his dear wife, whom we love) we should leave.

So, brush the chip grease across the denim of your thigh and goodbye, Candy Run. Drive, for chrissakes, and roll the fucking windows down. At the crest of the ridge, turn off the headlamps and holler a *Praise be to the crushed siderail that keeps us from that sweet beyond.* Test your memory of curves with a stub finger wrapped around the loose wheel, smell the coal spilling from the seam of the cut-through, navigate the turn by that chatter the dead make.

And while we're at it use the stars for whatever stars can be used for, and whatever lightning bugs can be used for let them be used for that as well.

You Can Destroy This if You Want

[This a hammer.]
[This a mood.]
[This a soft *hahh*.]
[This a nothing-flower cursing them significant brothers.]
[This a cartwheel of increasing pains, dancer, dancer.]
[This a hard place to sit still.]
[This a moment when no one claims me.]
[This a mix of all that.]
[This then some.]

Rituals to Kiss the Saint of Understood

Dear Sister of the Resurrection,

That clip does little to keep the stray hairs from your eyes. You are a body of milk glass—sheen and glow upon the tended vanity. I had been wanting to ask you, when they come for you, will you leave me behind? Will you please? When the dark clay no longer accepts you? The prayers have stopped my ears, have bled into a room of faint echoes. The afterlife will find its satisfaction in some fashion, I suppose.

And forgive me,
A

Sestina for the Wide Awake

The honeysuckle calls in the predawn light,
the low buzz drifts through the open window, winds
into my sleepless ear. This spring it has wound
near the pathway, choking the old stone
wall. In the new morning its scent calls out
and is answered: a love song

of sorts, because of its sweetness. Our love songs
are so different, we could not recognize them in this light.
They could not survive such diffuse illumination. Out
there the day wakens. In our bed the thin sheet winds
around our twined legs. The stone-
gray sky will soon break, and bleed like a wound.

I have not yet slept, too wound
up, unable to quiet the needling of thought spurred by the song
of a lone train's whine at two thirty a.m. The calved stones
of the valley reverberate, the low golden light
of its passing illuminates the tree line which winds
between here and anywhere. Because I am awake, I let the dog out,

and the dog goes because he wants out.
He has been sleeping at my feet for hours, a sock wound
around his frantic dreaming paws. The wind
carries the new spring honeysuckle like a song
into the room to wake him. Put out the light.
What keeps me from sleep pools like a stone

bruise beneath my skin. Or, like a worry stone
I thumb, every regret plays itself out,
wearing a groove the coming daylight
fails to fill. Each wound is an old wound;
each new song repeats the refrain of an older song
which is never a lullaby. Nothing darkens a window

like the mere thought of a darkened window,
though common sense says this is not so. The stone
wall, beneath spring's abundance, cracks. Songs

of morning birds flit along the valley. Out
there: no guarantees for the length a wound
might take to heal itself. In a while, the daylight

will fully reach, fully unwind itself. Out-
side my dog pisses on the stone wall and the vines wound
into its aged mortar. So much for song, so much light.

Dear Empress of Raze, of Slash, of Burn,

I had not called you. I had been thinking furze and brow when I met the man, but the light was not right. I was unable to see what he carried in his hands: it was neither cup nor fog nor spear of filigree and spun glass. *Dearest, dearest, dearest,* he said. He had a mouthful of *thous*, a mouthful of cinnamon, which he pressed against whatever might accept such kisses. His shadow weighed more than his shoes. *Precise love*, he said.

You must be kidding me,
A

Gibbous Moon

Because where we are no stars reflect,
(With no lip of light, without the full moon to define, to adequately
define, the path's edge, and the ravine we try to avoid—)

we become a void of stars;
(why not believe other lights might could guide us?
The light that emanates from each honeysuckle tongue)

we break the surface tension of stagnant water, piss warm from August
(breathing sex, the light of us against the other, flint in the dark cup of hand,
or the quick line of freeway lights, at least, which shimmer against

whatever they can.). The only way to distinguish ourselves is by lack.
What happens here has no witness, and
if we are quiet, only our breath will disclose us.

In the shade of this tree, against which my back is now pressed, no harm
comes to anyone, but do not mistake it:

this is no light our bodies can sustain.

Greenup Lock and Dam Road

[She was, last night, a hum.]
[Agin the hills bouncet back.]
[And forth the echo.]
[Swelled it.]
[Gived it back.]
[As a low.]
[Note from all.]
[Directions at oncet.]

Then she, *What don't take you shores you up*
[making the sound of a mouth ajar with want]. But
he only hears night jars churning.

Dear St. Matthews Church,

Who is not mailing me today with good news from our lord and savior? A stack of sealed prophecies lay in a milk crate stolen from the IGA. Paper sandals and blessed pennies, holographic Jesi and felted prayer cloths, open-eyed mirages, letters beneath my pillow to call all them saints; I dream of suffering and wake to lovelessness.

Somewhere in this I should create a room for god. And then all wonders will be revealed?

Give me time and many mercies,

A

Blacklick Creek

I.
She moves near the water-edge, not knowing the cause of alarm raised. What she does know: the creek bed is several degrees cooler than the fields of parched corn rimming the town; no one is walking there; the trees beg for rain with leaves cupped; gnats swirl near the carcass of a rabbit felled by her own paw; she is not meant to be part of this swelter.

II.
Because there is a *because* everyone begins to behave differently: in the town, on the edges of the town, we move deliberately; at the bar we cease to share a smoke outside the door at close; at home the dogs are called in quickly: suspected movement in the windbreak.

III.
Lazy in the sun we want her, dark among the reeds stalking late summer fawns, in unmown median. Something to break new interest into a day dull with humid exhale and draw, a new report, some sound bite on the local: lion, prank, coyote, rumor, unconfirmed, sighting, sighting, sighting.

IV.
She is following the basin of Blacklick as it oxbows along the east side: behind the mall and strip club, marking the edge of corn and soy fields, near the evangelical church, the landlocked new subdivisions: "Something Harbor," "Something Cove."

V.
She is sighted. Sighted in the low rise of July corn, in the clear cuts of wetland separating sprawl from sprawl, and near the trestle of no train still running. Few of us imagine her long sulk from West Virginia— something about fascination.

VI.
We do not focus on the road as we drive the short distance between our town and the next; we scan the fields and each gold-tan rump of a grazing deer staggers us momentarily; we hope for the snaking lion's tail to drag across our periphery. We want: movement in the corn, a gap between the row moving endlessly, to infuse the dry rustlings of drought with life, to break time into factors: pre- and post- extraordinary.

VII.
Officially, it has been seen once by the fire department en route, twice by policemen, and several times near the creek. Unofficially, one woman saw it sunning in the clear-cut space between field and shelter-break on Rager. She did not report it to any authority save her own mother. She did not want to guess at the weight of the animal, nor describe the stretching of its spine, or its wide afternoon yawn. But she did turn back to see it disappear into creek-side weeds: pokeberry and sumac.

VIII.
Maybe it came to break the stages of our lives, encapsulating them so that they feel full of something. The pale freckles that pattern my sister's cheeks emerge in the summer sun; the lion disappears under foothills of speculation.

Dear Shameful,

Brokenness ain't a color you'll recall like the drooping heads of flowers; there is no storm blossoming on a split stem bright enough against the wet earth to represent it. If it were a texture like salt, it would be salt. Or it would be bright quartz sand rolled against your calf, flecked with small flower buttercup, and stretched along the creek side.

Ain't no saint for understood,

Golden

Rituals for the Exorcism of Ghosts

Three Locks Road (Deadman Crossing)

Although the fruit grows heavy and bright,
we do not eat with the dead.

We do not eat of the dead:
their jewel-brightness, ripe for the taking.

We leave the fruit of the dead:
it rots on the grave where it lands,
we remember what feeds it.

Loss as Mars

    April 6th 1997

When Mars became Mars, dreaming died in the red dust;
those bright fields in the telescoping eye
unbecoming fantastic. Shudder and toss off all that
possibility. That you in absence are.

That night the earth was all shudder and weep;
we looked skyward. And not at the track.
All of us driving in the purple night,
dreaming sky, half asleep to the road.

The wind: green hay.
The low radio: lost to crickets.
Things will converge—I will not sleep
and you will die.

What we understand on the far side of the horizon
changes the reality of where we stand.
Mars is a disappointment in relation to the idea of Mars.
The window to my bedroom will be open all night.

The fan will mask, as it does, the sound of the train.
When it passes me, blasting its quick warning,
five miles east you will already be dead.
And your eyes, like brown pools

staring deep into the dark that conceals you,
will change into something not you.
Mars stays put. Gone the dream of canals.
Things become things again.

The bright whorl of universe, abstract and symbolic, fixes itself.
I see you not. You fall away.
Into possibilities stranger than the field
you are shelved in. Mars, in its orbit, predictable, barren—

cold sister, cold twin, dying for a glass of water.

I scrape from you a hollow to fill with adoration.
I walk out into a morning heavy with pine, and there
the warm hollows of your neck—

the scar your indistinct hand makes in my body.
One afternoon I realize I am older than you.
Mars is Mars.
I sleep to the retreating sound of electric fans.

I gather clover on your grave
and chain it. I
picture grey in your hair. I feel your
laughter beneath the yellow

leaves.

Something Else in the Snow

For Logan Lee Beery Babbert

I cannot stand the sound of trains waking me: I blame you.

                The absence of leaves tastes acrid.
They practically poured you in a coffin. A photo propped on the closed lid.
A picture of your dog on the stone.

                You smelled like snow in summer.
Your neck was ozone.

All the tiny burn holes in your shirt said heat. Read heal.
You are a cut leaf. A fire bug.
The cold metal track.

Your mouth   *I watched fireworks on your grave in July.*
was always cold.   *Read Agamemnon on your grave in September.*

The only dark line in winter is the cut of the track.
Having nowhere to run, I ran to you.
My god, you were bitter.

You are a boy in cold water, frost edging your lashes:

a boy coming in from the cold. Or a footprint
in fresh powder.   *In November I can taste the ozone.*
I knew when you left a room.

Dear Mother of Weakness,

A boy who never begs, a boy like a siren, a boy like a tree, a boy mudhungry and riverwashed, a boy unafraid, a boy whose hum is the sound of retreat, a boy who calls the bones in the earth to rise, a boy who licks salt from rocks he places on his tongue like the names of saints in litany, Selah, a boy whose mouth is a blur and a sneer and a honeycomb of psalms, a boy who is always the dark against the dark in the distance, a boy whose stationary body blocks the spilled yellow light of all windows, a boy with fingers juice-stained and nails dark with dirt, a boy who forges charms to send rain, a boy who sings cicadas from their shells—let him not come for me.

Let him not arrive in the night.

Let him not haunt me, that brown-eyed boy.

A

Bridge Road

Six seams will thud against the tires—
know: once you cross this river there is no
going back. Things will wither,
others will explode in mad blossom.
There will be buds on trees
you cannot put a name to.

Orpheus Road

Not even the despair of the open-mouthed flowers,
soon-to-die, at the side of this road rimmed
by rock and the sleep of water,
fissures of grit and slick and shale collapsing,

can purchase the dull, flat weight
of shame from me—a man I loved
is flake by flake unbecoming, talking backwards
as he halves and halves forever into fragments
I bury where he can't be found.

Houston Hollow, Long Run Road

My brother is a variegated trillium and
                I am dying of beauty.
The cut of his lip is sparked
in beauty. What is dark in him is dark
in me, and I would pull it out into
                            the world.

Sometimes a great calm bears me, and I have the sense to listen.
The sound of the river changes at
night—
                the shoreline frames a thousand tiny moons
                  rising in the still water—
the close hills echo nothing.

And I love, here, where flesh
is uncertain,
in the tangle of sleeping woods
        I untie myself in vain from.

We are what we are:
filled with ambiguous tenderness.
We are drawn of water,
        moon, dark bramble of rose,
        the shadowy form I work to compose—
my slow hands in adoration twined.

Please, skillfully, strip from this life this life.
        Strip it of all things still and bright.
We are full of shadow and sleeping light.

Magnolia, Salt and Pine

I am in love with the heat gathering in the eaves
and what moves from my stepping feet.
I try not to spin in the front yard in a dance for rain.

The dark comes early.
It is 9 pm on the top of the hill and the bright clouds
        roll across the state line.
It is 9 pm here and soft dusk drops with spent needles.

How long before we decide it is night?
Because at two am the sky is a smoky purple, at four it oranges up;
dawn is blue and resin-heavy.

Even moonless, the sky is light through the pines
whose lines extend, threaten to kiss
above my head on a distant plain beyond
        whatever sky arrives.

And when they're all backlit and glitter, a cathedral,
their shimmy is the texture of all things.

The old light of stars seems like a threat;
the jangle of legs and wings that strike
and grind is not music,
        just bodies
            in their ripe exoskeletons.

A fine mist dulls the gloss of magnolia which, except in spring,
is ever composed of separate darks.
One leaf shadowed by
        all leaves shadowing each other.
Beneath the velvet backs of leaves: egg sacs, patient bodies.

In the dark, things move.

The smell of dirt in the air smothers
the notes of exhaling flowers, except
the honeysuckle, magnifying all weakness.

I fall asleep in the yard.
I dream of salt. I wake up crying.

Rose of Sharon: What Stays

> The eye of him who sees me will behold me no more; while thine eyes are upon me, I shall be gone. As a cloud consumed and vanished; so shall he be who goes down to the grave. He returns no more to his home, nor does his place know him any more.
> Job 7:8

Wake up, there was something I needed you to remember, something I told you. Wake up.

First, there was the dream of god.

Next, came the dream of drowning.

Then, then, came the dream of—

I took the long way home, drove hours along Seven, scenic byway by scenic byway. The river still, deceptive.

For a long time I could not sleep because if I did someone else would awaken and undream me. And I, nothing but suggestion, would dismantle mote by mote.

Where the freeway used to end, it continues now, cutting a bright swath. Following nothing.

There was the hard pain of you. And everything I cherished, dismantled.

I slept, but my heart was awake.

Between the driveways the Rose of Sharon bloomed in crepe purples, in damaged pinks.

Some things stain: fallen blossoms, bitter dye.

The petals we gathered from the ground smelled of rainwater, of the slight pickling of a dark stream: the acid clay, the backfield of tall weeds.

They smelled of nothing which is the opposite of being.

Of straight ruin.

We pilled them between our fingers, and the darkness in them, that darkness—some things stain, Golden. Burst out wet beneath the rub of our skin.

The long way is preparation. Map-less, after years, I find you.

And if a word has, as we suspected, power, if it has that, then the stain on our skin, as we dyed ourselves savage, that stain stays.

Wake up, I need you to remember the word. What we spelled.

>Your first word was *light*.

And yours was a long time coming. Maybe damn, maybe mine, but I remember whole sentences that poured out of you all at once.

But the thing I need to remember—

>Was not *return, return, oh, brother, return to me* like water moving.

Wake up. First, there was the dream of god: no halo, no fanfare. No sacred heart burning for every sin. And what he asked of me, what he asked me not to forget, I had forgotten upon waking.

Would you fix your eyes upon me?
What would I do if you didn't want me?

Next, came the dream of drowning, and you, a great weight tearing.

I think of you mostly in rain. We huddled against the screen-less window of our room, wrapped in a quilt of ridiculous color. Your left hand beneath my head, your right hand embraced me.

>Make your bed.

I think of you mostly in rain. Our mothers would be furious, everything sheened in a room of sleeplessness, as I pressed my face to the cold cling of your hair.

>   Light the light.

I think of you mostly as rain. I dreamt my body was the muddy roll of water along the Scioto—I dug what I could into the bank. I clutched at everything, but still spilled beneath the rising.

At one end of the valley the sky darkened; we watched it come. Out on the Run the asphalt softened, nearly hissed.

>   Don't you know you can't come home?

My body cupped like a leaf to the rain to hold you.

In my wallet, among receipts, a grainy photo: your hair dull as dry grass. A crease runs along your cheekbone.

The diesel on the road rises like steam. The oil is dark on the trestle.

I dreamed the banks of the river at night. I dreamed alone. I dreamed the pressure of so many blossoms, the bright skinned fish flashing. I dreamed lead weight into my body, the cast and whirr.

I dream you white as dredged flesh. And beneath your skin, where I cannot see, little fissures forming.

Scattered blue light is the glare on the water hiding that which is beneath the glare—the unbroken water.

The dreamt moon, no bigger than a grape, is lit from within. You break its tight skin beneath your tongue and it spills out golden.

Bright mirror come touch a copy of you. Press to the point of fracture. Portions to all takers.

>   But, first come first—

I am an aperture set to slow. I keep your upturned face, bright cataract, colorless in the dim dissolve. I wear you thin beneath my adoration. An image like an Our Father. What shall I beg of you?

I dreamed I was twin boys; one could not speak, so neither spoke.

I forget our voice.

The rain tastes of copper, of blood, or wells it will later touch. It works a prophecy to itself. Or it tastes of the memory of your hands, cupped, pruned, and the tongue which laps.

There is such silence when the storm gathers, when the clouds, when the dark thunderhead peeks above the ridgeline— alto cumulus, brontide.

I am an aperture set to mourning. Negative superimposed upon negative. Are you imagining me?

The dark center wherein no pain diffuses, nothing shatters, nothing rises, or drifts like a rain of bitter blossoms.

We are more like many ashes falling. I need you to remember.

    Blackbird, bye, bye.

Selves In Memoriam

I.

Do we wake in blue light and pick up the baby?
What worries were born then?
        What shames brought forth?

In a small room the dresser
        is overflowing,
the grit of the floor roughens everything;
keys turn the tumblers as he leaves.

I expect the dishes, I expect
the phone will ring,
        carrying the voice of our always hopeful mother.

Everything is fine.

Small bottoms in small chairs, and tender love;
nothing wrong with tender love,
        who would not want tender love?

And weekends and evenings filled
with quiet
        laughter in a
                too small space.

Wheedle away the small monies
from small successes;

plan an hour
beside the window,
        potted fern,
a book no one would expect us

to find such tender love in.

II.

In the artist's studio
we bend our head to the oak display case.

The UV lights illuminate everything:
        we need to see the truth of things,
their angles, highlights.

Even if we settle on beauty,
        we still settle.

What is stowed in careful boxes?
        The lily
        curved against an unfocused dark,
        the bowing wing of what bird,
        the red gleam of hair that sways
                before the bending form?

Bright swaths of light draw the eye
        back
into the field.

We work the canvas in thirds,
        mark each trinity for what it is,
                for what it can do.

A good brush holds its shape—sheds nothing.

The filbert is an outstretched palm,
        mimicking the movement of leaves against sky.

The still lives
        bloom
                in careful rows.

III.

In the bright kitchen we will mourn the death of love.

A night at the bar
is every night at the bar,
and every night is at the bar:
      with or without us.

He tumbles into bed; his dark eyes
near-black in the dead of night,
      his dark hair a shadow,
           his wet mouth a sweet siphon.

It is sweet to forget:
      the smoke in his hair,
      the sting of him,
      the rough and smooth of him.

If there was something more we wanted,
      he made us forget.

There will come a day when everything will shatter,
      everything will burst forth and rend.

Even his bones will splinter and shame us.
Even in the bright kitchen, we will hear
      the cold metal twist.

Every train will be the same train tearing through the same night.
      We will mourn the death of love.

The rest of our days a hard swallow
      against remembered pain.

In Amber

Because of you cut pears smell boozy with decay.
Brown sugar glues to itself in the bowl.
The past flows like pine and maple.

And this is why I repeat the rituals for to call down light.
They are a stopper.
                     They do very little.

I need a bypass for the cabochon lodged in some ventricle.
In the long run I'll need a new pump—this one is always breaking.
There was a stint of dreams that worked like aloe to stay the pain
burning my fingers
        sequentially as musical notes,
while I slipped my tongue along the far edge of worn memory
reshaping it into some sweetness lick by lick.

And like the owl says: *the world may never know.*
Because the temptation to burst the seeming permanence of
days into nothing is so great that it sets our teeth to worry.

You take up an unfair share of space.
Specimen in glass gathering no dust.

There in the amber pane. Distorted, magnified—
the once remembered,
                          once brim with blood.

Divination Road

Then here you are, come round, thinking I owe you
        what? Saying *The dead are unreliable.*
And *Get in the car and drive.*

In the cold light of the rearview,
your eyes a cave of wet leaves against passing lights.

You profess the unreliability of the dead,
but here you are, fifteen nights straight
        with your work boots on.

What the dead dream is
spelled in light on the mud-dark water
and mapped in elevation.

And those dreams? Less oracular than mundane:
        take out the dog,
        thaw dinner,
        pay the man what we owe,
        because we do owe.

Twenty-eight miles of mineral silence
before we hit the river road lit
        like a skein of tinsel; one wants

a night of stars for drama's sake.

If I wake in the driveway
        staring at the three-quarter moon,
if I wake in the front passenger's seat of my car
        frosted over with cold,
or in the kitchen and you've tracked god-knows-what in
        from the other side,

battering my heart with that strong sense of up and leave,
        what might you expect of me? *Baby, get in the car and drive.*

Rituals for to Call Down Light

Rases' Mountain Road

Here is the end. Here. In early light this could be an island.
This could be anywhere. Trust nothing you cannot see—cannot touch.
The blued mist fills the bowl of the valley. Is there a world now?
Why would you even care?

Judas Codex

> Step away from the others and I will tell you the secrets of the kingdom.
> *The Gospel of Judas*

Everybody's hope is that somebody leaves.

    Everybody's hope is that somebody leaves.

I woke to the sharp smell of rain. Outside, the forsythia crumpled, the daffodils bent their mouths to the earth. I am so far from you. Wherever you are peonies already droop on their green necks.

There is no better life here.

    You run from or you are ruint by, Blackbird.

Everyone will call me a liar, but what each of us remembers is different. And maybe I elaborate more than another, but what of it?

What is acceptable loss? You should be here with me.

    And leave all this?

I stood at the counter cutting green onions, lamenting the sweet dirt rush of ramp that I lack; it grew wild on every embankment, wild in dense clay. The breeze can't carry the scent of ramp and honeysuckle where there is none.

You should be here—with me.

    I don't belong; you belong; you can change.

But whole sentences poured out of you. Look at the way you understood the stars.

And I said: *I will not be your hungry ghost.*
    And Golden: *I ain't your dark double.*
And: *Look at what you've given up.*
    And: *Look what you done left, love, look it.*

History's most famous kiss is betrayal.

What was on your lips?

    ...was nothing important.

And where I come from? We never make it back there.

    It weren't there. You done gone crazy.

Your lips are a seam of scarlet. I am hunger-bitten.

    How long will you torment me with words?

Don't you quote scripture to me, brother. I know how wickedness spills sweet in your mouth.

    Prove me a liar.

    Oh, baby, ain't you under my same skin, same skin.

You carved no heart, save in your heart for me.

    You turned and gone: you just up and gone: what ought I to do? Come run after, fool?

Am I your sacrifice?

    I'm your sacrifice?

There are always more sacrifices than we know.

Prima affectio...

    First love.

See, love? You *don't* belong here.

    Love, *you* don't belong. What are you doing here, Blackbird?

Sorrow Road

The moon illuminates the clay of the field—
the dark gathers and moves in the threshed rows.
The bodies of deer, grazing in the pre-dawn,
roll and turn indistinguishable against
the shelter breaks.
Here, silence only pretends,
                      and spills out.
A man—only darkness, his shadow drags the ground
perpendicular to the light. I read his body on a dim
page. He carries nothing. I know, in the coming
light, not even bent grasses shall bear
witness of his step.

Mid-Afternoon: Everything Darkens, Everything Bows

The rasp of rain splits, by drops,
the dark swelter of August, and beats
the already heavy leaves into the earth that bears them.
It comes as heat and the hiss of pavement below
the wheels of passing cars. The afternoon
grows dim, suspect—things diffuse.

>Well, let it come then in sheets that drip
their way into a quiet room and lightning
that shakes the frame of unlit windows, and let
it break such branches that are meant to break.
The soft maples groan and now
pressed by water, they scatter limbs like lives,
in all directions. Then, the rain
will push a softness into every single edge.

Shoreline

There is nothing more sacred than those
        who, in the thick of desiring, despair completely
              at anything.

In the dark he shifts between her and the luminescent numbers of the clock.
        Are *they* love poems? Are they the way we kiss each adverb
              in a search for clear water?

At five a.m. she will move
        from the blue light of a computer screen,
              straighten her gown strap

and stretch
        beside her sleeping husband, her sleeping dog, to dream
              of a river which pants

at the edge of its embankment, her ankles
        in the silt of the Ohio, the track
        undercut.

Sometimes she forgets: this morning, her mother's address,
        her father's birthday,
        where and when

to bring a covered dish. She remembers how to gather though,
        to surge and draw back
        again.

One night they came to the river to adore each other.
        Now she is a river turning against itself
to claw the edge of its embankment.

She turns her head,
        searches for the coolest part of her pillow.
              Anything can be washed away.

You Did Not Seem the Boy

The river is twenty percent silt, sixty sorrow,
and the body of a boy, swept near the grist
in the loop current there.

There is an issue of trust. I trust you implicitly.
I allow you to wrench the skirt from my hands,
and, beyond the mud-thick shoreline, lead me.

A few other things seem important: darkness,
for one. Nothing lighting the
wear of your, now our, consistent bodies.

You walk the path regular as any constellation,
bank to bank with your own curvature. So, I trust
you: *Come in. It's not too fast.* But his body

like yours, was slight. No one led him in. I
imagine his lip's pale kiss against the slate bottom of the river.
It gets slick in the middle here. No one held

his hand like you will hold mine, in the next few
seconds, eager as a child to show me how
swiftly we are carried downstream, half-naked to

anything. You are a boy who does not leave. Nothing
is ever as innocent as our bodies delivered back.
We rob one another of nothing.

The long folds of my skirt spread, we lay back
in the dry grass, oblivious to the night
and what moves it—in it. I might have been afraid

otherwise. I might have been so many things.

Acknowledgments

Thanks to the following journals and presses who published many of these poems in their earlier incarnations:

Anderbo: "You Can Destroy This if you Want," "Greenup Lock and Dam Road"

Beloit Poetry Journal: "Three Locks Road (Deadman Crossing)"

Cimarron Review: "Judas Codex"

Swamp Pink (formerly *Crazyhorse*): "Something Else in the Snow"

Fall Lines (The Jasper Project): "Candy Run"

Greensboro Review: "Ties"

Indiana Review: "Blacklick Creek"

Lit: "Dante Vena's Dog"

Ritual no.3: For the Exorcism of Ghosts (Stepping Stone Press): "Houston Hollow, Long Run Road," "Gibbous Moon," "Bridge Road," "Something Else in the Snow," "Rose of Sharon: What Stays," "Desire Road," "Selves in Memoriam," "Divination Road," "Judas Codex," "Races Mountain Road," "Sorrow Road," "Mid-Afternoon: Everything Darkens, Everything Bows," "Shoreline," "You Did Not Seem the Boy."

Riverwind: "Sestina for the Wide Awake," "Shoreline"

Sonora Review: "Boneyfiddle: Floodgate"

Tampa Review: "You Did Not Seem the Boy"

The Carolina Quarterly: "Ridgerunner," "Dear Mother of Weakness."

The Pinch: "Communion Road"

The Poetry Center of Chicago's 14th Annual Juried Reading Chapbook (Dancing Girl Press): "Dear Empress of Raze, of Slash, of Burn," Dear Sister of the Resurrection," and "Dear Saint Matthew's Church."

Amanda Rachelle Warren's poetry and non-fiction has appeared in *Tusculum Review, The Carolina Quarterly, Appalachian Heritage, Anderbo,* the *Beloit Poetry Journal,* and other journals. Warren received their masters in creative writing from Ohio University and their doctorate in creative writing with a focus on poetry and Appalachian literature from Western Michigan University. Their chapbook, *Ritual no.3: For the Exorcism of Ghosts,* was selected by Kwame Dawes as a winner of the 2009 South Carolina Poetry Initiative Chapbook Competition and was published by Stepping Stone Press in 2010. They are the 2017 recipient of the Nickens Poetry Fellowship from the South Carolina Academy of Authors. They teach professional and creative writing at the University of South Carolina Aiken with their colleague/partner Roy Seeger. *Rituals for to Call Down Light* is their first full-length collection. The collection grapples with place (literal and metaphorical) and its corresponding struggles, traumas, triumphs, and joys.

www.ingramcontent.com/pod-product-compliance
Lightning Source LLC
Chambersburg PA
CBHW020340170426
43200CB00006B/450